73

Write About an Empty Birdcage
a collection of poetry

ॐ

by Elaina M. Ellis

Write Bloody Publishing
America's Independent Press

Long Beach, CA

WRITEBLOODY.COM

Ellis, Elaina M.
1ˢᵗ edition.
ISBN: 978-1-935904-28-1

Interior Layout by Lea C. Deschenes
Cover Designed by Joshua Grieve
Cover Illustration by Lily Lin (Berlin)
Proofread by Jennifer Roach and Sarah Kay
Edited by Jamie Garbacik, Courtney Olsen, Alexis Davis, Sarah Kay, and Derrick Brown
Type set in Bergamo from www.theleagueofmoveabletype.com

Special thanks to Lightning Bolt Donor, Weston Renoud

Printed in Tennessee, USA

Write Bloody Publishing
Long Beach, CA
Support Independent Presses
writebloody.com

To contact the author, send an email to writebloody@gmail.com

This book is for Jessica Joy.
Thank you for holding on to you & me.

This book is for Peggy & Alan Ellis.
Thank you for holding on to each other.

WRITE ABOUT AN EMPTY BIRDCAGE

WRITE ABOUT AN EMPTY BIRDCAGE

WRITE ABOUT AN EMPTY BIRDCAGE

ADVICE FOR THE NEWLY SINGLE

WHAT I WISH FOR AT 11:11

WRITE ABOUT AN UGLY ANIMAL

WELCOME BACK

Write About an Empty Birdcage

WRITE ABOUT AN EMPTY BIRDCAGE

Write about an empty birdcage. As in: write about your
ribcage after robbery. Use negative space to wind a song
from the place on the dresser where a music box isn't.
Write about the corners where the two of you used
to meet. Draw the intersections. Arrow to the side-
walk where her shoes aren't near yours. Write about

an empty birdcage. As in: write about a hinged-open
jaw that is neither sigh nor scream. Use this to signify
EXIT. Be sure to describe the teeth, the glint of metal
deep down in the molars, the smell of breath after lack
of water. Draw this mouth a thirsty and human portrait
of what it means to be used up. Write voice by writing

how it feels when it's painful to swallow. If you must
put noise in the scene, make it the sound of bird wings
flapping in a cardboard box. Take hope, and fold it
small as seed, then suck on it. Slow and selfish.
Write about an empty birdcage. Birdcage can read:
building, structure. Abandoned, or adorned. As in:

loop and tighten a vine of nostalgia around the room
you currently brick yourself into. Recreate the sweet
of jasmine, but mortar the door so it will not seep
through. Write about an empty birdcage. Replay us
the scene. As in: she presses her pale cheek against
the window, as he turns his pinstriped back, slow and

final. Again. She presses her pale cheek against the
window, as he turns his pinstriped back, slow and
final. Again. She presses her pale cheek against
the window, as he turns his pinstriped back, slow and
final. Write about an empty birdcage. Write about
the hinges. Describe them as dry knuckles. Write

how I became a moan.

Go

And so it was
that I packed in my suitcase
a magnifying glass, a negligee,
and a butter knife. Tools
for a month-long journey.
Stepped out with my legs half-
shaved, raspberry lips,
alarm- clock
swallow.

And so it was
that I left for some time,
slept in the shelter of car wheels
and freak-show shacks. And so it was
that I pressed my lottery-ball-popcorn-machine belly
against the bellies of strangers,
asked them to feel
my baby kick.

And so it was
that I studied my skin
and the skin of the sidewalk.
How are we similar,
how are we different.
Creamy, blemished me.
Asphalt, perfect it.

And so it was
that I became a scientist,
that I became a condiment,
that I became — .
Spreadable. Lamentable.
Precise.

And so it was
that the calendar days
origamied into blooms,
and I convinced myself it was spring,
until the recycling truck turned everything
into something else again: branches to bones
to silk and sticky glass. It was bright white
mornings and siren afternoons.
Wind your toy engine.
Ready,
set,

Prayer for My Partner's Lover

Your name is lovely,
stark and brightly hued, soft
nape to harsh click, in the span of two syllables.

In my mouth you are a collection of sounds.
In his mouth you are a new home. At night,

he carefully spits out rubies while he believes I am asleep.
He shines them for you while he does his laundry.
He keeps one long string in his pocket,

so he can necklace you
when the time is right. I am thousands of feet
above streets and houses, as I write your name.

I am in the patch of sky traceable by Oregon.
Did you know that's where I'm from?

The sharp of those evergreen trees
and the edges of seasons, round, that you eat
like new fruit: these are the natural angles

of my bones, the curve of my fat hip.
Did you know my father near-left my
mother, the year before I grew breasts?

He was still wearing an overcoat, the morning he told us.
The heat of my sleep against the cold of his coat.

The new woman had a name like yours.
I never wanted him to kiss me again.

I saw your face and body on a poster once,
tattooed and dewy. I took the poster down,
brought it to him, watched the flush begin

at the base of his neck. As I write this, I am
thousands of feet above the electrical poles.

I imagine the corners of every city are papered
with your name. I am praying hard for
the merciful shake of a windstorm.

After Kneeling

Get up off your knees. Sit down at the table.
Baby girl, it's been too long since you've
had something good to eat. Let Mama
cook you something warm. Let Daddy
rock you. Baby girl. You deserve
a full plate.

Get up off your knees. Sit down at the table.
This is your home now. This is your home,
and these are your bones.
They deserve to be draped in curves,
deserve to be upright. You need
shelter. Let me shelter you.

Get up off your knees. Sit down at the table.
It's time to look me in the eye.
Those eyes should not be wasted on dirty tile.
Look at me.
Look at me.

Get up off your knees. Sit down at the table.
The big boys are playing. You can do this, too.
Pull out your swollen   words.
Your large   ideas.
Slap them down, make them pay.
You deserve to win this round.

Get up off your knees.
No more gulping down his pleasure.
No more hiding your smile.
No more cleaning his floor with your grief.
No more secrets. No more
secrets. Baby girl. Come sit next to me.
Come sit down at the table.
It's dinnertime.

HEIRLOOM

There is a loose strand of inheritance
called appetite. I have pulled it slow

from the hem of my mother's skirt.
She is unraveled, but see —

it was not hers to begin with.
Let us pray.

Our Fathers, who emptied the shelves
so we could not get fat,

hollow be thy names. See
how I am still eating.

I have smashed down every quiet bit
of plate and glass from the cupboard.

Off-Screen

We were all each other had left.
That is not entirely true, but
in the dim drama of one bombed
moon, we held on as if our future

had popcorn-greased itself out from in-
between fictional crib bars. As if our maybe-
babies had slipped, wriggled all the way off-
screen, into a world where scientists

blow up romance on the regular. This ouch
was nothing new, really. It was just a quick
rip of loss, as the bottoms of our
shoes stuck to the Coke and candy muck

of the floor, while the image we'd held onto
floated to ceiling. It was just that suddenly
things had become literal. The movie
physically swallowed itself back

into its own long dusty tunnel of light,
cannibalistic, as story retracted to machine.
And then? We were the only
lungs in one dark theater,
caught in the throat
of a breathy embrace.

HANINA'S LETTERS

I.
A friend once claimed she saw my hair spell words
in wild cursive on the pillow, while I drooled on into sleep.

A poet, even when you snore, she said. I said, *I don't snore!*
She said, *Metaphor.* I said, *Right. But is it true about my hair?*

Then I thought...it makes a certain sense:
the burning bush that is my hair, my hair that curls
because I am a Jew, would speak a burning word
or two out of the desert of my sleep. *Oh,*

this is is deep! I said. She said, *What?* I said, *Exactly. What?*
What are we, if not poetry of family tree?

She said, *But,*
I said, *What?*

She said, *What language did your hair leak onto pillow?*
I said, *You tell me!*

She said, *See, you were spelling fast. I didn't think to ask.*
So I said, *Language of the past!*

You know that Jews read backwards, right?
She said, *Books read right to left?*

I said, *Yes, time-travel style!*
She said, *We are in the future?*
I said, *Yes, and my hair is in the past.*

She said nothing. I said, *Hair is in the past!*
She just laughed and said, *I'm out. This is too queer,*

and then she passed out on the couch. I watched her hair
for minutes in the moonlight. Straight as grass. Silent
as dew. I twirled my curls and sighed, *it's true. It's queer*
to be a poet. A poet and a Jew.

II.
Two thousand years ago, a teacher called Hanina
preached Torah. Tender. Always blushing,
as if it were a letter from a lover. Meanwhile,
the Romans roamed the desert, arm in arm
destroying all things Jew.

        Hanina's friends warned,
They're coming for you, but still the Rabbi read sweet
messages from G-d, until the Romans found
a vestige of his teachings. They caught him,

        reaching thirsty toward the heavens,
pulling stories from the text. The Romans told his students,
watch this lesson, while they rolled him up in Torah,
and let a slow torch take the scroll. The students

        cried, *Hanina,*
please, what do you see? The Rabbi called, *The parchment,*
it is burning. The letters are flying

        free.

III.
Sixteen years ago, I left a love-note on the bathroom counter
in my parents' home. It was folded, like 8th grade notes were folded
back then. My mother found the note, unwrapped my secret,
and read it back to me from memory. I cried. Denied. Swore,

I'm not gay, we only play like this.
Don't want to kiss her, like I said!
Eww, no, don't want her in my bed,

and Mom just shook her head, then recommended therapy.
I found the note and burned it later (they can't prove
what they can't see) and we didn't talk about it again 'til I was 23,

but all that time, I knew they knew me.

Here's the thing:
despite the shame, I was relieved. The paper had burned,
but the truth was out there, flying free.

Rabbi Hanina: I am embers. I can feel that's nothing
new. It's queer to be a
poet,
            to be a
poet. A Jew. It's queer to be a
poet. To be. To be a.

                    to b

                                    e .

To Be.

Heirloom II

A woman in love with her hunger
is an accident scene.

Grandmother, look! There is blood
in my cake.

TORCHED SONNET

Jealousy (that old peculiar ghost) leans
bones against the bar: mahogany,
an obtuse door from Old Hotel. She sings
her torch song; loosens robe. Tears negligee.

She moans a dirty moan: thick, filthy bathtub
ring. Her collarbone circles the room, sways
brooms and mops in ill-fit shoes. We hiccup,
        One more round!
She ropes, *You monsters! Say*

'Please.' — spools ribbons from our roughed-up lips,
then gestures with her nose, a sharpened spoon.
We're cut! All praying muddy drinks, palms ripped.
She mounts the grand piano. We plead, *Croon*

another nightmare, Mother Mean!   She leers.
He wants her more than you. Marry your fears.

ADVICE FOR THE NEWLY SINGLE

ADVICE FOR THE NEWLY SINGLE

Be a fierce-dragon lonely-queen,
Emma. Be a drunk, barren

crowbar. Be a cocktail-waitress, heart-sewn
tease. Be a desert plant, Susie.

Succulent. Need no water at hand.
Be an empty-fridge, sale-salad

scrimper. Be a sharp-tongued solo
chef. Anna: watch TV on a lonely moon

through the static of milky way
reception. Concentrate

on falling asleep. Slut,
Mona. Slut your book open.

Keep your legs open.
Do not write any name but
your name on those acre-wide
pages. Be hollow,

Sally. Keep canary-singing
in a thirsty well. Be a singing

flighty bird with an open beak.
Don't try a cushion,

Mary. Don't swallow soft.
Chew only sticks: carrots, twigs.

Sit on your bones.
Sit on their bones.

Don't try for dreams.
Don't try for dollars,
Leah, this is a coin job
for you. Turn out the light.
Tear out your eyes.

HOLES

There are those that we fall in.
"We" meaning: women starring
in romantic comedies, or rather
starring in the loose cinematic
loop of our egos.

There are those we literally
fall into: potholes in the middle
of the street, our skirts flying up,
over our heads. Our hair
flying up, to heaven.

Our screams flying up to the mitt
of a man, who wraps them around his
wrist to hear again later. And we fall
into what: the city sewer?
We never reach the bottom.

We just fall like pretty things
should fall. It's all about a quick laugh
and then the show
of our panties: either polka dotted
or shamefully plain, baggy.

And then there is the flash
of fear: our eyes filling like plates,
our mouths pursed like whistles.
Upsidedown in panic, wondering
(how) will this end?

Although, of course
we've seen it all before.
Which means: a tall man
will throw a rope,
sooner or later.

CHANGE IS A DEMANDING LOVER,

and I don't mean simply that she'll sit on top and ask for
more than you think you can give, although she'll do that.
And you will thrust harder and go longer with her than any
somebody should: when you have to work in the morning,
when the neighbors might wonder, when wives and
husbands are waiting for wayward spouses to come home.
Sweating this much for this many days in a row can't be
healthy, you will think, and you will ask, where is a glass
of unsalted water when I need it? Where is the person I
used to be, and why is the mirror shaking when the piggy
bank is standing still on the dresser? If this isn't an
earthquake then what kind of freak beauty is it, exactly?
And though you will be more thirsty than Noah was before
the flood, you'll find you've forgotten things you once
needed: how to hold on, for example, and how to swallow.

To Glow in the Dark

This is what girls with bodies
                              must do from time to time
            or every day: rotate one arm all the way around
itself. Rotate one neck away
      from the mirror,   toward the mirror,
                                    away, away, away
                  from the mirror.
Girls with bodies
                        must from time to time
            remove one mascara tube from
one inner ear;   apply armor. Must stand
                                  on the scale for fifteen
                  minutes, or until a lead snake
      slithers away for cooler grass, leaving one
            pillow feather waiting to be eaten
                        by flame,
                                          or not.
            This is what girls with bodies know
they must do from time to time
                        or every day: hide
                              the matchbook:
            third drawer down, in the belly
                              of the jewelry box
                  on the shelf, above the Tampax.
You know, this is what girls
with bodies
                        must do from time
                  to time   or every day: lower one
      fistful of confections
                  into the toilet,   or
                  a bucket of gasoline.
                        Hold one hand
above sea level,
            like holding a tongue

or a
                              boy; it is a thing. A thing
                                             to be kept.
Girls with bodies
                                        must from time to
        time   or every day
                                 roll two eyes all the way skyward.
            They know they must
                              tremble, tremble,
              with a slick ever-readiness
            to glow in the dark.

FEMME ON FEMME

When tasted we are: too much sugar.
When fingered, we are:
too much wet.

You and I,
we are supposed to be
repulsed by each other.

Since I was a little girl,
I wanted you to cross the classroom
to talk to me.

Grab my sticky hand. Lean
your forehead toward mine —

I used to tell stories about men
sneaking in my room at night
to steal my childhood. I wanted you
to climb inside with me and my doll-friends,
where our syrup would turn to crystals,
and we'd shine there: safe
and powerful and young
and desired.

How many afternoons
will I let the delicate shadow of lace
spill quietly under the table?

I dreamed the sweetness
of mirror-ball sugar cubes
would dissolve slowly under my tongue
while I curtsied, deep in frills.

Tantrum

I do not have to be the daffodil,
pursed in mouthy song for pouting boots.
I do not have to fold back my collar,
cheer up any damp neighbor with the gold
of my naked neck. It's true I am a trumpet
of trumpets. It's true the sunny coins of summer
early shine at the back of my tongue.
I do not have to pay out in yellow,
hold throat open for the tickling.
    I am a swallowing fish.
    I am my own clinking bank.
    I am the echo of riches plunking
    in my own fat storage.
I do not have to preen for vase,
or flinch away from rough thumb-to-finger grabs.
I do not have to be a gift for grabber's lover
or lover's mother.
    It's true I am a value of values.
    I am a rich fist pressing open to deposit thirst.
I do not have to be a bulbed or gulping sentence.
    I am a reaching open,
    I am a bobbing treasure.
I do not have to be a flash of bright around the corner.
I do not have to stand on any corner
I've not chosen for my own.
    It's true I am a decoration.
    See the pleasing brilliance of the hand I horn
    from page to page.
I do not have to be a brief thing.
    Hear the long, round sound
    of my own call?

Dear Mr. Sunflower Butch, Growing Tall in the Parking Lot of My Apartment Building,

I'd like to take you on a date.
I'm not the kind of girl who wants
to pluck you from your boots,
stick you in a vase, call you hers
for some short week. Call you pretty thing
while you twist and twist and twist

your neck toward the window. While you lift
your stubbled chin toward your father.
While you stubborn-sing baritone yellow
until the thirst is too much for your throat.
Until you can't remember, suddenly,

what kind of treats you used to dig into
with your now-gone toes.
I'm not the kind of girl who wants
you nodding, shiny Mr. Dapper
when the guests come around,

shriveled when she goes out of town.
Mr. Tall Sunflower Butch,
you deserve to stand how you stand
and get all that you need. See,
it's just I'd like to put on some short dress

and bring you water. Nose my admiration
up on tiptoes, right into the bowl
of your righteously seeded mouth.
When I say I'd like to take you somewhere,
I don't mean away from here. I mean,

Mr. Sunflower Butch, stay right tall
while I show you some chivalry:
while I reach past your shoulder
to tickle that fine neck. While I stroke
your petals with no urge to pluck.

If that's too much, I don't need
to touch you. I'd like to stand back
amongst the cars here, and the bugs,
and the neighbors. I'll just stand
in the parking lot, to appreciate
the length of your spine.

MAGNOLIA

There is something so tight about those buds on those trees
across the street. Something so cupped. So: fingertips
pressed tight together. Secret. Erect. New, and green at
their base. There is something honest, but something
dangerous, there. Like hunger, held tight. Like all of youth,
held tight. Like naked. Like invitation.
Like watch me. Like watch me.

And I do. I watch them. I watch
their pink-tight expressions.
Sometimes I almost whistle. Sometimes I say, Damn.
I am so turned on, as they are so turned in. Damn.

There is something so loose about those blossoms
on those trees across the street. Open on the tree now.
The size of open palms on the tree. Deep lipstick stain
on white teeth. I am taken with these sweet floozies, but I
wonder already when they will fall apart. I see petals
swaying breezily together, holding soft, like teenaged girls
link fingers. Casual.

There is something so loose about their beauty.
I don't think it will hold them through the afternoon storm.
I'm not sure it will last them through the season. There is
something so open-mouthed about those blossoms
(laughing) like, catch me! like, catch me!

Wish I could cross the street with my own mouth open
wide, wide enough to swallow each foolish girl-petal as she
falls. Instead, something goes winter in me. I do not cross
the street. I lose my appetite. I turn my eyes away. Let the
sidewalk hold out cruel arms.

Mmm, mmm. I shake my head. There is something so sad
about those blossoms, and something so tight about those
buds.

WHAT I WISH FOR AT 11:11

What I Wish for at 11:11

:
I want
a fat blue bird
to keep me awake at night.
I want a room full of her loud
blue rustles. I want a fat blue bird
to shake and shriek her fat blue body
truly through me. I want fat
mouthfuls of feathers,
pillows stained
blue.

THAT ONE

There was once a wizard who bent time
      to make room for me on her mantle.
Her cologne was incense and plum
      juice, sweet and strangely crawling.
Early afternoons, she took me down from in
      between ceramic figurines and whispered
scenes from Legends of the Fall into my ear,
      slow, until I slept, pressed into a pillow
of grass. In the night, she made breakfast:
      one scrambled egg for me, over-easy
for her, served in dreams and always real syrup creep-
      ing slowly along the pancakes. Mornings, I woke up
next to her falling, caught her with the meager
      cushions of my breasts, and we made love like that.
In the under hours, the dog-eared times of day, she
      wrapped me in paper bags and sent me to to sea,
where I solved riddles and shivered. There I most craved
      her warmth, missed her neat arrangements
of things in the living room, the way she
      squinted one eye at the broken
clock, to measure me clearly.

B-Poem

A house full of clocks:
I want to mourn out loud.
I want to mourn out loud

in a house full of clocks
full of hours
of days
of years
seeking a safe place to turn myself
inside-out without being discovered.

★

I want to be discovered.

Locking doors behind me. Turning on
faucets to drown out the sound.
Removing coat and gloves and sweater
in Massachusetts winter. Removing

shirt to protect my image. Leaning
over the edge of smooth porcelain bowls.
Leaning over the edge in public stalls.
Leaning over the edge in friends' bathrooms,
in my own home, with the shower turned on.
Leaning over the edge while I was supposed to be in class.
Leaning over the edge in high heels. On holidays.

After I swore I'd never ever again.

★

Watch me become a backward image- sequence
in a better movie. Here, the broken glass moves from the carpet
where it is embedded, piece by piece back to its original form on the bedside
table. While night moonwalks to morning, watch bits of seeds
blow against the wind to nestle back on their dandelions.

In other words I want to talk about vomit,
but I want to take it back
before you can smell gluttony
or illness on my breath.

*

What I'm saying is political.
Age four, learn: a girl gets hit
when she opens her mouth, and worse
when she opens her legs. Age ten,
learn to look down at your thighs and sigh
with disgust. Age twelve, learn:
a man wants a housewife
half a mother's size.
I want to testify
about the bingeing. I'm afraid
you'll think I'm a pig.

I want to say this,
because we are not pigs.

*

We are not pigs:
I'd swell my belly up good
with fear of my own power.
I would eat and eat. I ate. I
ate until I couldn't breathe.
I went searching for a door to lock
behind me.

I'd lean over that porcelain bowl,
and this is how the private performance began:
I'd lick two fingers on my right hand, or run them
under the faucet to make things go smoothly.
I would stick them good into my throat,
and I would beckon like a dyke;
it was sexual.
It was my art

and my sport
and my sex
and my shame.
It was my poetry.

★

So see how
instead of lingering in my lover's bed,
in my tile temple,
on my knees,
I would beckon in slow, wide circles inside
my throat, until it opened. Until saliva came.
Followed by rushes of liquid
splashing into the bowl, onto my face, forearms, bra.
I would cough and coax, until more
came. I would come
until my knuckles were raw
and I was empty
and spent.

I have spent hours
of days of this life
cleaning up after my own
vomit. Cleaning public
toilets, with shaking hands.
Wiping somebody else's shit
from the rim of a bowl,

caked underneath
my wet mess. I am

hours of days — a wet
mess. I am wet —
a mess. I want
to mourn out loud.
I did this.

OCTOBER

In October, a pumpkin gets
desperate. Hands reach in to
pull orange innards away from shell.
Flesh goes stringy, clingy, releases
a scent that is humiliatingly sweet.

It all gets scraped away. Fists,
fingernails, spoons with teeth.
Storied gist discarded in favor of still.
In favor of a smooth clean wall
and empty eyes and gaping mouth.
Now pure enough to sing candlelight

into goblin eyes. I wonder if we gutted
us too soon. Or, I wonder if there was
another way. Not so hungry for hollow.
Not so impatient to illuminate.

Sometimes, sweetheart, I dream about
those neighborhood bully pumpkin-
smashers. I dream they steal our gourd,
and smash it to comforting bits.

Dear Toilet,

I've been meaning to write you this letter for some time. Of course, I often start letters and never send them, and I'm too cheap to buy stamps when I can just e-mail, though I don't have your e-mail address and I'm not sure if you're on Facebook.

Toilet,

I trust your judgement precisely because we had such a romantic relationship back in the day, always searching each other's watery eyes for the answers. Let's be real: I was more than a little bit bloated back then, wasn't I? Even as I shrank, I was all popped blood vessels, and puffy around the neck. An insecure wreck, and it showed. Along with the half-digested food that stuck to my clothes, it showed.

Dear John,

Help me make this story funny. When you have something like this all over your hands, you have to laugh about it. I have to laugh about it. And what are queers good for if not to turn tragedy into camp, closets into cabarets, potties into muses?

Honey Bucket,

I'm fierce today, am I not? With curves and a voice to show for it. Did you ever see me in heels this hot, back then? No way. This is survivor's flair. And we got here together. Just thought you should know.

xoxo

Dear Geraldine,

My bow tie is crooked for you. The paper I write on
is yellowed with leftovers, and the top drawer full of dust.
The pot on the stove rattles and I won't remove it,
until your rows of false teeth curl again like twin slugs
on the night stand.

Your face is a marigold: cheap bobble of nature.
All afternoon I have wished to snack on goldfish crackers,
although they are not particularly delicious. See?
I am still a greedy fist for your cheese and carbohydrates,
mimicking the quick crumble of our conversations.

I want to tell you, your ear is a hermit crab: an ugly muscle
in a generic shell. Your ear is a hermit crab
and I invite you again to crawl clumsy close to me,
appall and entertain me with the strange shape
of your listening.

And your nose. I remind myself, your nose
is a troll under a bridge. The bridge itself is no miracle
of architecture, but it is a lovely — if dangerous —
stroll from the glare of your one bean eye to the squint
of the other.

O, bring back your many failures, the flat dirt of your
tongue, the rude earthen squeeze of your chest. I miss even
your wheeze, the sigh of a flattening tire.

Yours.

P.S.: Your voice, as I recall it, is a light bulb. Harsh glow,
and then the sad crunch of broken filament. Let me
unscrew your disappointment and we'll start again,
attracting swarms of godforsaken moths to the artificial
sunlight of our love.

CLUCK NO (A TERZANELLE REFUSAL)

Many evenings now, you've heard me lock latch
behind your cluck. Many evenings, I've heard
your bike shoes down the stairs, their eager clack.

You wheel away toward another bird
who'll take you into nest. I turn on lamps
behind your cluck. Many evenings I've heard

the flutter of your knuckle- knock advance,
apologies. And pecking, now again:
Will I take you into nest? I turn on lamps,

light up my desk, the room. I call my friends.
Tell me I should ban him from this breast!
No apologies. No. Won't peck again.

But there you are again, helmet to chest,
clucking loud. Bright earnest wing, creased face.
(Tell me I should ban him from this breast!)

Many evenings now we've skirt-chased
one more time around the tree. Hear that latch?
Cluck loud, bright earnest wing. Turn that creased face.
Walk bike shoes down the stairs. Click-click, clack-clack.

CONFESSION, AFTER EVERYTHING.

When my body finally said yes
to women, it was a muffled-in-
muff yes. It was a suckled
into nipple-after-nipple yes.
It was a loud popping yes,
wet yes, red yes, yes after years
without. I almost didn't think
of you at all.

Is/Is Not

A collarbone is not a bench for you to sit on.
A collarbone is not the collector's necklace or
a fainting couch. A collarbone is not a swing-set
or a ladder. Not a church beam, not a high
wire at your circus, nor a string between
two cans.

A collarbone is not a pool-side curb.
Is not the grace of baby grand piano swerve.
Is not a mantel for your candles or a floorboard
for your letters. A collarbone is not the creep
of coral underwater. Nor an edge of blue
in winter's gray. Is not the headboard
of a bed or the lock on a door, the car's bumper, nor
your sailboat's mast. Is not a handrail.

A collarbone is not a dog bowl or
a tide pool, nor a thimble's tin.
Is not a promise or a daisy chain.
A collarbone has never been a back-porch
or a bottle lip. Not a diving board's bounce
nor the chattering of teeth.

A collarbone's not telescope nor
constellation. A collarbone connects one
shoulder to another and a cage of ribs
to a long white throat. Is body bone.
Is marrow: mine. Is not a headline or
a snapping branch. Will never be
a perch for your bright bird.

WRITE ABOUT AN UGLY ANIMAL

WRITE ABOUT AN UGLY ANIMAL

Write about an ugly animal.
Go to www.ugliestanimalsever.com
and snag the ugliest of all
ugly bodies to write about.

Skin an ugly animal
and make it your beautiful
puppet. Skin an ugly thing
and make your cold self
a coat.

Skin an ugly thing
and chop her lungs into
your lunch. Consider
throwing a dart at the woman
who stole your beautiful

baby. Instead, write,

> *There is something too*
> *ugly about the ruination*
> *of a beautiful thing.*

Digest an ugly lunch,
and never think of _____ again.

> *On the corner of 18th and*
> *Union there is a couch inside*
> *the coffee shop. The couple there*
> *is the droop of a Tom Waits*
> *song.*

Admit that ugly things aren't
as lonely as you. Wish to be
an ugly thing with many pocked
friends.

> *They are dressed*
> *like wilting. I don't believe*
> *he will ever let go of her*
> *skin-dripping elbow.*

Claw apart your hair and face   Ask to be stripped
of your petticoat.

> *On the corner of 15th and Spring*
> *a park bench remains where my*
> *skirt does not. The tango of his*
> *flattery was red and orange polyester.*

Write about the ugliest sex you ever had. Pray to be cast
down from your pedestal.

> *He told me I was*
> *the most shimmying*
> *sheen in the*
> *world.*

Lope about your apartment, now frenzied
like the ugliest jazz. Wish this was funny. Know
this is serious.

Admit that you miss the ugly
smell that used to linger around the room.

Write about http://transcendence.

EXCERPTED LETTER TO THE STAR-NOSED MOLE

Dear Animal,

I hope your eyes burn hot above that nose anemone.
Freeze bully boys mid-grab,

with all the fire of your wrong shape.
Freeze boys with the horror of your permeability.

>Though he is young, he sees her as
>an inside-out midnight disgrace.
>He laughs at her, with all the fear and loath
>in his boy heart.
>Oh, the kicks he gets. Because the star-nosed mole
>looks pusillanimous.
>Embarrassed on itself. All genitals for nose.
>All wrong-sized claws,
>sharp as stars, fat as drowned fingers. All tender
>flesh and bounce.
>Bully boy, he sees ripe fun. He takes her
>for a tease, a trick, a toy.

Dear Animal,

May you become Medusa amongst
mollusk-grubbing mammals. Oh burn
your taunters. Laughable, powerful you.

LISTEN

Boom it finally goes, when it goes: the drop of all that
waiting, weighing about as much as your mother's first
elephant-print dress, or rather as much as my sister's first
whale. I left the following on your porch: the word "lover,"
which you hate. A brass pineapple, a shovel. But it's more
of a thwack, isn't it? It thuds when it goes, more
of a bruise than a bleed. That's what I like, now,
finally more oomph and less missed mouth.
Along with your set of scrimshaw in a wooden box, I left
you an audio tape to explain. You'll hear the bang- roar
of suitors who wreck me better than you. They know
how to dinosaur my jungle only when I give out
the code: and the code is, I like it like,

PROPOSAL

Because a breast is not
a hand, but you can hold it. A breast
is not a dinner roll. A breast is not a napkin
ring or crouton. Yes it is. Because a breast
is not a baby bird, but cup it! Precious.
Because an angry mother bird is a red breast,
not quite a mouth, but you can feed it.
It can't feed you. Yes it can. Because a breast
is not an apple, but it's fruitful. An apple's not
a ring but you can shine it. A cup is not
a doorbell. Yes it is, when someone's home
to let you in. Because a wife is not a breast,
but you can stroke her. Yes I do
because a breast is not a door,
so marry me and be the hand
that bites the ring
that feeds you.

Horizon, One Morning I Watched You

as you split yourself open again,
candied yolk again, spreading again
across the day. I was hungry,
and that felt selfish.

I felt sorry in 365 languages,
for all the ways in which you
will never say no.

Later, for breakfast,
because no one had come
to feed me, I peeled
a perfectly pink grapefruit.
I pulled its parts apart.
I pretended forgiveness
for the sticky give,
one section after another.

Isn't there a kind of violence
to the inevitability
of sunrise?

WHAT IS TOO HARD TO WRITE IS THIS

: the twitch of my wrist still wants
to flip to a grab or a fix on your
fist wants to grip to the gulp
of your go: two is better than now
one is want, too is wrestling ask
from your flask is that sweat
beading rude on my brow? give
away is hot sweet is not bad is not
bade me farewell is not well is not
fair is stairwell is sex is as sex
does press me cornered and swell
is your swollen my woolen is
gone down the stairs would they
stare if they saw our see-saw
would they saw our in two
into a halved peach on the beach
is just sand in my sugar, just sssh
guaranteed to be mess to be sss
to be me is to mess spill the beans
on the floor on the beach be
the ache in my wrist in my wreck
in and out of my jeans billy jean
you're not not my not my
not my lover.

HEIRLOOM III

Lord, there is shine on my chin
from the breakage.

Slow down to watch me wreck
what is and isn't mine.

HALF-WAY THERE

Swing now, we're up
and out of the darkest part,
pale as paper and thin.
See our pockets sag
with treasure from
the digging.

Proof of where we went
and where we didn't go:
on the bedpost, discarded
nightgown. In the closet,
emptied shelves. On the desk,
abandoned bank statements.

In the bathroom: apologies
on squares of toilet paper.
And prettier things, too.
A new comb. Teeth we thought
we lost. Night-blooming
flowers.

On the radio, one song
repeats, implies we should be proud,
implies we're looking forward
to the stretching out of day.
As if a longer mouth
will be easier to feed.

IT SHOULD BE SAID
THAT WE LOOKED GOOD TOGETHER

There was that one day at the beginning of things,
when I wore my bright green long-sleeved v-neck
t-shirt, and you wore your bright blue new hoodie,
while I walked brown boots next to the whir of your yellow

bike wheels, and your handlebars were orange.
You'd brought two apples, called Pink Ladies,
but we were no ladies: you were a boy in a gray
speckled cap, and I was a girl with black bra-straps

showing and slipping, so we stepped and rolled bright
against the bleak of 12th Avenue. We took blushed bites
of March as if it were ours to swallow, stopped. Red,
to kiss. Stopped, denim, to sit on a stoop. Stopped, silver

so you could pull a mix CD for me from your messenger
bag. The volume at which we laughed was neon. Not
electric, but shocking, the way the vivid of rhododendrons
is inappropriate against the concrete of a city

afternoon. The itch in my palms to touch you
might have been what a green shoot feels like,
just before it allows a purple flower to climb
up on out of its throat. It was a feeling of near

burst. Oh, you were a boy in the rhythmic click
of your bike shoes, and I was a girl in the soft
of my cotton. We leaned cheek against cheek, against
the brick and bloom of the season.

WELCOME BACK

WELCOME BACK

Take off your gown of gone.
Wayward girls will not be punished,
here. What is naked and glad again
is not a shame. Believe it or not,
there is no need to keep a dark garment,
once it has lost its shine. You can look over
your shoulder, sure, but go on.
Put on a new record. That whistle
you hear is not the kettle, it is your own
long letting out of breath. Welcome home
to skin that wants you. Welcome
to your own lit room, perfect
for the party.

When the Time Comes

Unsnap your fingers. Undig your shovel.
Loosen the snug of your laces.

Unzip your skin: you will be cold at first,
but then you will be a burning field.

In the morning, be dark waters.
Become your coffee. Be first spill.

In the office, talk with your elbows.
In the meadow, be the sunset, held sigh.

In the bathtub, breathe with your fins.
Capsize the boat of your rage.

Go dancing. If your knees ache,
remove them. When your cheek heats

to hurting, offer it slow to another cheek.
Ignite there. When the time comes,

unpin your dress. Flame
your ego until it rises.

Up Up Up

The heat of the day
has a fist full of dandelion heads
and is ringing the doorbell,
but nobody's
home.

Above it all,
the hot air balloon
of my trust
has sailed languidly
(no one was watching),
up up up
into the turquoise
mouth of some one
else's dream.

When I Stop Writing Poems for Him, My Hand Will Probably Fall Off

I'm going to miss my hand.

One Night

O summer stars I can't see you but O I know you, Out the
window you rectangle Over and under the moon. I know
electricity is Only a network of veins that run O they run
from your hot heart. O summer stars your hot heart has
heated this city; we are burning. O summer stars I can't
hear you but I know you're O you're singing. Sirens, I
know, are Only the wailing we do when we can't hear you.
We echo your volume as the cricket echos the orchestra,
together we are a field of crickets and we are rubbing,
rubbing, and rubbing for you in this city. O summer stars I
can't taste you but I know you're hard- candy carmel, I
know you are sweet and O I know you are bitter, too, the
dark side of flavor, O you sing the burnt apology after a
breakup. O summer stars you are an apology after a
breakup. You are late, you are hard to find, rectangle
Overture, you are bittersweet noise. But then you are a
blanket of sincerity, O you are winking with all the sex in
your hot heart, you would not leave, you will not, tho I
can't see you O you are staring at my breasts tonight, O
you inconsiderate stranger, you intimate light bulb, O
summer, O O stars.

WIFE

Do not pull a single shade.

If the sun will be out in the morning,
let me meet her. If she has done the work
of heaving her great body hand- over- hand
from the well of night, up into my third story
window, let me be ready to say hello.

Let me offer ointment for her calloused grip
and let me greet her, thirsty. Let me be grateful,
uncloaked, and stretched as a canvas. If she
should spill this way, I hope she stains me.
Do not cover me with your own shadow,

nor down blanket, nor terry- cloth robe.
Understand this. I will rise this way
in the morning from my half-shell,
whether you are deep in sleep,
or eyes-pried-open.

You will not move me from the hot glass,
nor wipe the soot of the sill from my chin.
And as I leave your side to kneel in front
of her muscular, miraculous suspension in blue,
just remember:

You are cool-grove lover. Umbra-other,
go back to your pillow. Let me drink this.
Let me wake here.
Go back to slumber.
Just remember: she is wife to me.
You are other.

Dear Forgiveness,

I made the pie
of blueberries and agave
with a pistachio crust.
I hope you will find it

delicious. This isn't bribery,
rather it's that I saw you
every day last week:
through the kitchen

window, I saw you out
in the yard, tending to rows
of green with such reverence
for squirming crawlers,

humming that plum tune.
Dear Forgiveness, you
were working without
a handkerchief, no jar

of water. I should have
invited you in. I should have
offered a swig. A rest. Some
hospitality. That was last

Tuesday, but it has taken
me days to find a recipe
worth your company,
and then there were

the knives to hide. And
those drawers of keys
to turn upside down
over the compost bin.

And there was laundry
to do. I have been wearing
the same stained dress
all year. Dear Forgiveness,

here I am in a pair
of my own clean jeans
and this fresh apron,
which is to say I am

almost ready to ask for
your ear. I have placed
the pie on the back porch
to cool. I have washed

my trembling hands.
If you will sit — I hope
you are hungry —
we can begin with the eating

and the saying of things.
Dear Forgiveness,
the first slice
is yours.

BURIAL

Here lies our love, may it rest in pieces.
May it rest in as many pieces as there are
ways to tell the story. May we tell the story
as many times as it takes to get the wooly
sweaters off of our tongues. May we peel off
extra layers and stuff them into sweaty
backpacks. May we roll each other's sweaty
boulders back into shoulders. May we lick
the shoulders of the story so many times,
the words go pulp. May our tongues go pulp,
then clean as poles. May we stand clean
as poles and raise a banner to our love.
May the banner flap and rip above our
modest cemetery plot: here lie the rest
of the pieces. May they get to heaven
even though. Forgive us our stories
as we forgive the rusted toys
we'll walk on top of. May
we rest in please and
thank you. Please.
Amen.

Acknowledgments

It takes a community to write a first book.

Peer Editors:

Laurie Cox

Marita Isabel

Katie McClendon

Jennifer Morales

Tristan Silverman

Stefanie Fox

LaToya Jordan

Molly Metz

Corinne Schneider

Lane Stroud

University of Los Angeles Poetry Faculty:

Jim Daniels

Douglas Kearney

Richard Garcia

Carol Potter

Mentors:

Tara Hardy

Jenny Factor

And:

Ingrid Elizabeth

Tera Fukuhara

Tucker FitzGerald

Leah Wilcox Hughes

"Advice to the New Single" was originally published in *Muzzle Magazine*.

ABOUT THE AUTHOR

Elaina M. Ellis quit her day job in early 2010, to make poetry the boss of her. She is the founder of TumbleMe Productions, a Seattle-based vehicle for creative collaborations. Ellis is published in print and online, including *Push Magazine*, *Awaking Consciousness Magazine*, and *Muzzle Magazine*, and has been a featured performer on local and national stages. She is a candidate for a Masters in Fine Arts degree in Creative Writing from Antioch University Los Angeles, to be awarded June 2011.

Regarding bookings and other fun art projects, please contact the author at elaina@tumbleme.org, or visit www.elainallis.com and www.tumbleme.org.

New Write Bloody Books for 2011

Dear Future Boyfriend
Cristin O'Keefe Aptowicz's debut collection of poetry tackles
love and heartbreak with no-nonsense honesty and wit.

38 Bar Blues
C. R. Avery's second book, loaded with bar-stool musicality and brass-knuckle poetry.

Workin' Mime to Five
Dick Richard's is a fired cruise ship pantomimist. You too can learn
his secret, creative pantomime moves. Humor by Derrick Brown.

Reasons to Leave the Slaughter
Ben Clark's book of poetry revels in youthful discovery from the heartland
and the balance between beauty and brutality.

Yesterday Won't Goodbye
Boston gutter punk Brian Ellis releases his second book of poetry,
filled with unbridled energy and vitality.

Write About an Empty Birdcage
Debut collection of poetry from Elaina M. Ellis that flirts with loss,
reveres appetite, and unzips identity.

These Are the Breaks
Essays from one of hip-hops deftest public intellectuals, Idris Goodwin

Bring Down the Chandeliers
Tara Hardy, a working-class queer survivor of incest, turns sex,
trauma and forgiveness inside out in this collection of new poems.

The Feather Room
Anis Mojgani's second collection of poetry explores storytelling and
poetic form while traveling farther down the path of magic realism.

Love in a Time of Robot Apocalypse
Latino-American poet David Perez releases his first book
of incisive, arresting, and end-of-the-world-as-we-know-it poetry.

The New Clean
Jon Sands' poetry redefines what it means to laugh, cry, mop it up and start again.

Sunset at the Temple of Olives
Paul Suntup's unforgettable voice merges subversive surrealism
and vivid grief in this debut collection of poetry.

Gentleman Practice
Righteous Babe Records artist and 3-time International Poetry Champ
Buddy Wakefield spins a nonfiction tale of a relay race to the light.

How to Seduce a White Boy in Ten Easy Steps
Debut collection for feminist, biracial poet Laura Yes Yes
dazzles with its explorations into the politics and metaphysics of identity.

Hot Teen Slut
Cristin O'Keefe Aptowicz's second book recounts stories of
a virgin poet who spent a year writing for the porn business.

Working Class Represent
A young poet humorously balances an office job with the life
of a touring performance poet in Cristin O'Keefe Aptowicz's third book of poetry

Oh, Terrible Youth
Cristin O'Keefe Aptowicz's plump collection commiserates and celebrates
all the wonder, terror, banality and comedy that is the long journey to adulthood.

OTHER WRITE BLOODY BOOKS (2003 - 2010)

Great Balls of Flowers (2009)
Steve Abee's poetry is accessible, insightful, hilarious, compelling,
upsetting, and inspiring. TNB Book of the Year.

Everything Is Everything (2010)
The latest collection from poet Cristin O'Keefe Aptowicz,
filled with crack squirrels, fat presidents, and el Chupacabra.

Catacomb Confetti (2010)
Inspired by nameless Parisian skulls in the catacombs of France,
Catacomb Confetti assures Joshua Boyd's poetic immortality.

Born in the Year of the Butterfly Knife (2004)
The Derrick Brown poetry collection that birthed Write Bloody Publishing.
Sincere, twisted, and violently romantic.

I Love You Is Back (2006)
A poetry collection by Derrick Brown.
"One moment tender, funny, or romantic, the next, visceral, ironic,
and revelatory—Here is the full chaos of life." (Janet Fitch, *White Oleander*)

Scandalabra (2009)
Former paratrooper Derrick Brown releases a stunning collection of poems written
at sea and in Nashville, TN. About.com's book of the year for poetry

Don't Smell the Floss (2009)
Award-winning writer Matty Byloos' first book of bizarre, absurd, and deliciously
perverse short stories puts your drunk uncle to shame.

The Bones Below (2010)
National Slam Champion Sierra DeMulder performs and teaches
with the release of her first book of hard-hitting, haunting poetry.

The Constant Velocity of Trains (2008)
The brain's left and right hemispheres collide in Lea Deschenes' Pushcart-Nominated
book of poetry about physics, relationships, and life's balancing acts.

Heavy Lead Birdsong (2008)
Award-winning academic poet Ryler Dustin releases his most
definitive collection of surreal love poetry.

Uncontrolled Experiments in Freedom (2008)
Boston underground art scene fixture Brian Ellis
becomes one of America's foremost narrative poetry performers.

Ceremony for the Choking Ghost (2010)
Slam legend Karen Finneyfrock's second book of poems ventures
into the humor and madness that surrounds familial loss.

Pole Dancing to Gospel Hymns (2008)
Andrea Gibson, a queer, award-winning poet who tours with Ani DiFranco,
releases a book of haunting, bold, nothing-but-the-truth ma'am poetry.

City of Insomnia (2008)
Victor D. Infante's noir-like exploration of unsentimental truth and poetic exorcism.

The Last Time as We Are (2009)
A new collection of poems from Taylor Mali, the author
of "What Teachers Make," the most forwarded poem in the world.

In Search of Midnight: the Mike Mcgee Handbook of Awesome (2009)
Slam's geek champion/class clown Mike McGee on his search for midnight
through hilarious prose, poetry, anecdotes, and how-to lists.

Over the Anvil We Stretch (2008)
2-time poetry slam champ Anis Mojgani's first collection: a Pushcart-Nominated
batch of backwood poetics, Southern myth, and rich imagery.

Animal Ballistics (2009)
Trading addiction and grief for empowerment and humor with her poetry,
Sarah Morgan does it best.

Rise of the Trust Fall (2010)
Award-winning feminist poet Mindy Nettifee
releases her second book of funny, daring, gorgeous, accessible poems.

No More Poems About the Moon (2008)
A pixilated, poetic and joyful view of a hyper-sexualized,
wholeheartedly confused, weird, and wild America with Michael Roberts.

Miles of Hallelujah (2010)
Slam poet/pop-culture enthusiast Rob "Ratpack Slim" Sturma
shows first collection of quirky, fantastic, romantic poetry.

Spiking the Sucker Punch (2009)
Nerd heartthrob, award-winning artist and performance poet,
Robbie Q. Telfer stabs your sensitive parts with his wit-dagger.

Racing Hummingbirds (2010)
Poet/performer Jeanann Verlee releases an award-winning book
of expertly crafted, startlingly honest, skin-kicking poems.

Live for a Living (2007)
Acclaimed performance poet Buddy Wakefield releases his second collection
about healing and charging into life face first.

WRITE BLOODY ANTHOLOGIES

The Elephant Engine High Dive Revival (2009)
Our largest tour anthology ever! Features unpublished work by
Buddy Wakefield, Derrick Brown, Anis Mojgani and Shira Erlichman!

The Good Things About America (2009)
American poets team up with illustrators to recognize the beauty and wonder in our
nation. Various authors. Edited by Kevin Staniec and Derrick Brown

Junkyard Ghost Revival (2008)
Tour anthology of poets, teaming up for a journey of the US in a small van.
Heart-charging, socially active verse.

The Last American Valentine:
Illustrated Poems To Seduce And Destroy (2008)
Acclaimed authors including Jack Hirschman, Beau Sia, Jeffrey McDaniel,
Michael McClure, Mindy Nettifee and more. 24 authors and 12 illustrators
team up for a collection of non-sappy love poetry. Edited by Derrick Brown

Learn Then Burn (2010)
Exciting classroom-ready anthology for introducing new writers
to the powerful world of poetry. Edited by Tim Stafford and Derrick Brown.

Learn Then Burn Teacher's Manual (2010)
Turn key classroom-safe guide Tim Stafford and Molly Meacham
to accompany *Learn Then Burn*: A modern poetry anthology for the classroom.

WWW.WRITEBLOODY.COM

WRITEBLOODY
QUALITY AMERICAN BOOKS

Pull Your Books Up
By Their Bootstraps

Write Bloody Publishing distributes and promotes great books of fiction, poetry and art every year. We are an independent press dedicated to quality literature and book design, with an office in Long Beach, CA.

Our employees are authors and artists so we call ourselves a family. Our design team comes from all over America: modern painters, photographers and rock album designers create book covers we're proud to be judged by.

We publish and promote 8-12 tour-savvy authors per year. We are grass-roots, D.I.Y., bootstrap believers. Pull up a good book and join the family. Support independent authors, artists and presses.

Visit us online:

WRITEBLOODY.COM